POCKET GUIDE

contents

Map legend

▬▬▬	Free limited-access highway
▬▬▬	Toll limited-access highway
▬▬▬	Other multilane highway
▬▬▬	Principal highway
▬▬▬	Other through highway
▬▬▬	Other road
▭▭▭	Unpaved road (conditions vary — local inquiry advised)
··············	Scenic route
🛡190	Interstate highway
(183)	U.S. highway
(18)	State highway
43	County highway
⬜	City area
⛺	Campsite
🏕	Roadside park
▲ ▲	Mountain peak
‒ ‒ ‒ ‒	Foot trail

Park Locator Map . . . 2-3
Overview 4-5

Park Listings
Acadia 6-7
Arches 8-9
Big Bend 10-11
Bryce Canyon 12-13
Capitol Reef 14-15
Crater Lake 16-17
Cuyahoga Valley 18-19
Denali 20-21
Glacier 22-23
Grand Canyon 24-27
Grand Teton 58-59
Great Smoky 28-31
  Mountains
Isle Royale 32-33
Kings Canyon 34-37
Mammoth Cave 38-39
Mesa Verde 40-41
Mount Rainier 42-43
Olympic 44-45
Petrified Forest 46-47
Rocky Mountain 48-51
Sequoia 34-37
Shenandoah 52-55
Yellowstone 56-57, 59
Yosemite 60-61
Zion 62-63

Index by state 64

Editors
Laurie D. Borman, Brett Gover

Design
Donna McGrath

Cartography
Hans Anderson, Robert K. Argersinger, David Simmons, Steven R. Wiertz

Photo credits
©National Park Service — 7, 11, 12 (b), 20 (br), 24, 25 (tl) & (tr), 29 (bl) & (br), 33 (tl) & (tr), 34 (tl) & (bl), 35, 38 (bl) & (br), 46 (mr) & (br), 48, 49 (tl) & (b) 50 (tl), 52 (bl) & (br), 53 (tl) & (tr), 64;
©PhotoDisc 2003 — 4, 5, 6, 9 (tr), 10, 14 (tl) & (br), 16 (tl) & (bl), 18, 20 (tl), 21, 22, 23 (bl) & (br), 28, 32, 41 (bl), 42, 43 (br), 49 (tr), 50 (tr) & (br), 60, 62; © Corel — 8, 9 (tl),12 (tr), 14 (bl), 43 (bl), 57 (tl) & (b); © Rand McNally 44(tl).

Library of Congress Control
Number: 2003092800

For licensing information and copyright permission, contact us at licensing@randmcnally.com

If you have a comment or suggestion, please call 1-800-333-0136, ext. 6171, or e-mail us at: consumeraffairs@randmcnally.com

ISBN: 0-528-84482-2

Made in the U.S.A.
10 9 8 7 6 5 4 3 2 1

U.S. National Parks

1 Acadia
Located in central-coastal Maine

2 Arches
Located in southeastern Utah

3 Big Bend
Located in southwestern Texas

4 Bryce Canyon
Located in southwestern Utah

5 Capitol Reef
Located in south-central Utah

6 Crater Lake
Located in southwestern Oregon

7 Cuyahoga Valley
Located in northeastern Ohio

8 Denali
Located in south-central Alaska

9 Glacier
Located in northwestern Montana

10 Grand Canyon
Located in northern Arizona

11 Grand Teton
Located in northwestern Wyoming

12 Great Smoky Mountains
Located in eastern Tennessee and western North Carolina

13 Isle Royale
Located in northern Lake Superior

14 **Kings Canyon**
Located in the southern
Sierra Nevada, California

15 **Mammoth Cave**
Located in west-central Kentucky

16 **Mesa Verde**
Located in southwestern Colorado

17 **Mount Rainier**
Located in south-central
Washington

18 **Olympic**
Located in northwestern
Washington

19 **Petrified Forest**
Located in east-central Arizona

20 **Rocky Mountain**
Located in north-central Colorado

21 **Sequoia**
Located in the southern
Sierra Nevada, California

22 **Shenandoah**
Located in northern Virginia

23 **Yellowstone**
Located in northwestern Wyoming,
southwestern Montana, and eastern Idaho

24 **Yosemite**
Located in the central Sierra Nevada,
California

25 **Zion**
Located in southwestern Utah

An ardent conservationist, President Theodore Roosevelt was probably the most vigorous presidential supporter of national parks. "There can be nothing in the world more beautiful than the Yosemite, the groves of the giant sequoias and redwoods, the Canyon of the Colorado, the Canyon of the Yellowstone, the Three Tetons; and our people should see to it that they are preserved for their children and their children's children forever, with their majestic beauty all unmarred," Roosevelt said in 1905. During his terms in office, he signed into law the creation of five national parks and 18 national monuments (some of which later became national parks).

Today visitors have the opportunity to explore many parks and national monuments. This book covers 25 leading national parks, with essential information for researching and planning a visit. According to the National Park Service, the average park visit is just half a day.

With such a short amount of time, it's best to focus on one or two activities.

1. First, check the times and dates facilities open and close

2. Begin your visit at the visitor center

3. Decide which area of the park interests you and focus on that. Consider:

   • The main draw to the park, such as Old Faithful Geyser at Yellowstone

   • Enjoying the beauty of nature. Many parks have wildflower and endangered plant life programs. The National Park Service has a website and a hotline for wildflower information.

   • Looking for wildlife at certain times of year, such as elk in rutting season. Be mindful of safety, of course.

   • Trying out an activity. Take a hike, go on a horseback ride, paddle a canoe, catch fish.

   • Sign up for ranger-led activities. In season, park experts lead hikes, give interpretive talks, offer story telling, and much more.

4. Don't forget about your next meal—there may be a special venue in the park to enjoy scenery as you cap off a morning or afternoon in the park.

National Parks Passport information

For $50, park visitors may purchase an annual pass that admits a driver and all passengers into any national vehicle into any national park that charges admission. More than 80% of the proceeds from pass fees help support projects at the national parks. Visitors can order/purchase a pass:

- In any park where an entrance fee is charged

- At www.nationalparks.org

- By calling 888/467-2757

Websites:

www.nps.gov
One of the most informative sites on national parks, run by the park system. There you'll find tips and facts about each park, driving and weather information, news updates and much more.

www.nationalparks.org
The National Parks Foundation site also details information about the parks.

www.randmcnally.com
Plan a trip and learn more about what to see and do.

www.rangerfop.com
U.S. Park Rangers Lodge annually lists "ten most dangerous national parks."

By the Numbers

1	Number of national parks in 1872
56	Number of national parks today
84,426,961.02	Total acres of federal and nonfederal lands in the national park system in 2001
279,873,926	Total number of recreational visits to the parks in 2001—that's one visit for every person in the United States
286,382,054	Total number of recreational visits projected for this year
102.6	Circumference, in feet, at the base of the General Sherman Tree in Sequoia National Park
20,320	Height, in feet, of Denali National Park's Mt. McKinley
60	Number of summits higher than 12,000 feet in Rocky Mountain National Park
1	National park established to preserve the works of people, Mesa Verde
9	Average annual inches of rainfall in Petrified Forest National Park
150	Average annual inches of rainfall in the mountains of Olympic National Park
1,100	Cars broken into by bears at Yosemite in 1998

Source: National Park Service

In 1604, Samuel de Champlain spied Mount Desert Island. Not seeing any trees from his vantage point (though there are trees), he named it "island of barren mountains."

Acadia National Park was established here as a national park in 1919. Once a summer retreat for the wealthy, today's visitors still ride and bike on 44 miles of carriage roads punctuated by granite bridges built by John D. Rockefeller, Jr. Other popular activities include hiking up Cadillac Mountain to see the sun's rays first touch the U.S., walking along the shore line and tidepools, cross-country skiing and snowshoeing in the winter, or just driving the 27-mile Park Loop Road that brings together mountains, lakes, and shore.

- Located in central-coastal Maine
- General park information: 207/288-3338
- Hotel reservations: No lodging in the park
- Weather information: 207/667-8910
- National Park Service website: www.nps.gov/acad/
- Other website: www.acadiainfo.com

Best of Season

Spring-Rent an audio tour CD or tape from Hulls Cove Visitor Center and take the 27-mile Park Loop Drive. Begin early to avoid crowds and ensure plenty of time for various stops along the way, such as climbing to the 1,528-ft. top of Cadillac Mountain for a spectacular panoramic view, and walking along the shore at Sand Beach.

Summer-Call ahead to reserve a Wildwood Stable carriage ride by horse-drawn buggy along the roads built by Rockefeller. A one-hour ride circles Day Mountain. You can also charter a private tour (two-hour min.).

Fall-Mid-October tends to be the peak of the fall foliage season, when a riot of color bursts forth. Hike along the trails once trod by Native Americans and rusticators of the 1800s. More than 120 miles of trails cover the park—forested trails lace the interior of Mount Desert Island and Isle au Haut.

Winter-With the heaviest snowfalls in December, January, and February, and an average of 61 inches annual snowfall, cross-country skiing is possible throughout winter.

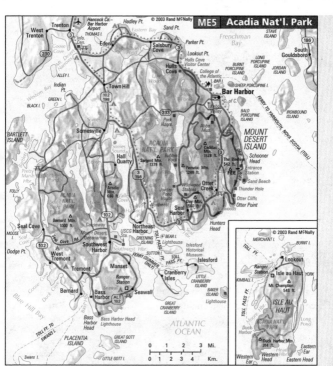

Cross-country skiing on the coast

Drive information:
From Boston take I-95 north to Augusta, Maine; from Augusta take ME 3 east to Ellsworth and on to Mount Desert Island. Or, take I-95 north to Bangor, Maine; from Bangor take ME 1A east to Ellsworth; from Ellsworth take ME 3 to Mount Desert Island.

Watch out for frequent rain and coastal fog.

More than 2,000 rock arches porpoise across Arches National Park. Formed by natural weathering, the arches range from three feet across to more than 300 feet. Some of their names describe their beauty and structure: Delicate Arch, Turret Arch, Eye of the Whale Arch, Landscape Arch. It is an awesome spectacle of nature, and one of the greatest density of natural arches in the world.

Native Americans once lived among these scenic wonders, and left pictograph and petroglyph panels carved into cliffs as evidence of their life. An 18-mile scenic drive (50 miles round trip including spur roads) takes visitors past many of the park's arches, with short hikes to the sites, including the petroglyphs.

- Located in southeastern Utah
- General park information: 435/719-2299
- Hotel reservations: No lodging in the park
- Weather information: 801/524-5133
- National Park Service website: www.nps.gov/arch/

Best of Season

Spring-Starting in March and April, the wildflowers bloom, making spring prime time to visit. The colorful show is best when there is decent rainfall, and flowers can be easily spotted by the road. Another good bet: Devil's Garden.

Summer-This is high desert, and summers are hot. Temperatures can exceed 100°F in the daytime, so join an evening program at Devil's Campground amphitheater.

Fall-Summer's heat is gone, and so are the crowds. Reserve in advance for a two- to three-hour afternoon guided hike into Fiery Furnace, where sandstone pillars poke flame-colored fingers into the sky.

Winter-Take the paved road to The Windows section, framing eight major arches and many smaller ones, then on to Delicate Arch Viewpoint. Delicate Arch was once known as Schoolmarm's Bloomers. On the return, a stop at Wolfe Ranch offers a glimpse into homestead life of the late 1800s.

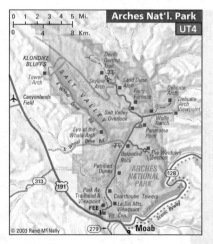

Delicate Arch; (inset) Wolfe Ranch

Arches Nat'l. Park
UT4

0 1 2 3 4 5 Mi.
0   4   8 Km.

KLONDIKE BLUFFS
Tower Arch
Canyonlands Field
SALT VALLEY
Wheel Drive Rd.
Devils Garden Trail
Skyline Arch
Sand Dune Arch
Fiery Furnace
Salt Valley Overlook
Delicate Arch
Delicate Arch Viewpoint
Wolfe Ranch
Panorama Point
Eye of the Whale Arch
Wheel Drive Rd.
Balanced Rock
The Windows Section
Petrified Dunes
ARCHES NATIONAL PARK
313
191
128
Park Av. Trailhead & Viewpoint
FEE
Courthouse Towers
La Sal Mts. Viewpoint
Vis. Cen.
Scenic Byway
279
Moab

© 2003 Rand McNally

Drive information:

The entrance to Arches is located five miles north of Moab along US 191.

Rio Grande, Chisos Mountains

- Located in the big bend of the Rio Grande, in southwestern Texas
- General park information: 915/477-2251
- Hotel reservations: 915/477-2291
- Weather information: Contact general park information
- National Park Service website: www.nps.gov/bibe/

Big Bend National Park flanks the U.S./ Mexico border, and is named for its position in the big bend of the Rio Grande. Its border flows alongside the Rio Grande for 118 miles. Mountains and desert tumble across its more than 801,000 acres, with more types of bats, birds, and cacti than any other national park.

The Chihuahuan Desert straddles the border here. It blooms with prickly pear cactus, claret cup cactus, bluebonnets, cane cholla, rock nettle, living rock cactus, ocotillo, acacia, mesquite, and many more plants from spring through early fall. March and April are the most popular times to visit because of the blooming plants.

Best of Season

Spring-Walk along the river for sightings of black-chinned hummingbirds, yellow-billed cuckoos, ladder-backed woodpeckers, painted buntings, even screetch owls and elf owls.

Summer-Take an easy early morning stroll on the Rio Grand Village Nature Trail and perhaps sight javalina.

Fall-Join a ranger-guided hike of the Chihuahuan Desert from Dugout Wells, or take a 1.7-mile walk on one of the most scenic trails, in the Santa Elena Canyon.

Winter-Low light pollution, little humidity, and infrequent cloud cover in winter is the perfect recipe for star gazing, with views sometimes as far as Andromeda galaxy, two million light years away.

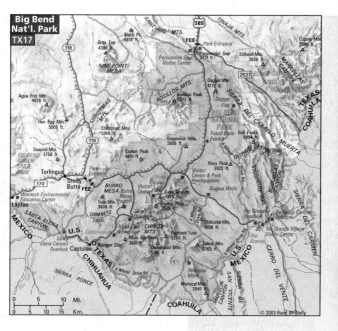

Big Bend Nat'l. Park
TX17

Hiking on the Window Trail

Drive information:
Several highways lead to Big Bend National Park: TX 118 from Alpine to Study Butte or FM 170 from Presidio to Study Butte (then 26 miles east to park headquarters) or US 90 or US 385 to Marathon (then 70 miles south to park headquarters).

The phantasmagoric shapes of Bryce Canyon, carved by erosion, are well-matched with a mystical name—hoodoos. These magical rock spires, jutting upward like the fluttering fringed edge of a blanket, form rock amphitheaters that glow with color at sunrise and sunset. An 18-mile-long drive along the Paunsaugunt Plateau rim overlooks much of this amazing rock architecture. At some points, visibility is nearly 100 miles.

Bryce Canyon has 50 miles of hiking trails that skirt the famous formations. You might spy a grazing mule deer, elk, or pronghorn antelope. More than 160 species of birds visit the park annually. Wildflowers bloom later here—often in the summer—so peak visitor season is also peak flower season.

- Located in southwestern Utah
- General park information: 435/834-5322
- Hotel reservations: 888/297-2757; 435/834-5361 (same day only)
- Weather information: Contact general park information
- National Park Service website: www.nps.gov/brca/

Main Amphitheater (below); (inset) flowers

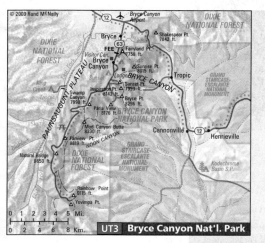

© 2003 Rand McNally

UT3 **Bryce Canyon Nat'l. Park**

Best of Season

Spring-Drive up to Rainbow Point, stopping at 13 viewpoints along the way. Some of the highlights include: Sunrise Point, Sunset Point, Inspiration Point, and Pink Cliffs.

Summer-Join a guided hike among the hoodoos under a full moon. Sign up early at the visitor center on the morning of the hike.

Fall-Join a cowboy on a 2- or 4-hour mule or horseback ride into Bryce Canyon Amphitheater along the Peekaboo Loop Trail to learn about the park geology.

Winter-A light snowfall sets off the color of the hoodoos and makes this the perfect time to cross-country ski. One of the best trails is a road the rest of the year, off the main road to Fairyland Point. If the snow is 18 inches or more, the visitor center offers free use of snowshoes to traverse the park.

Drive information:
From the north or south on US 89: Turn east on UT 12 (seven miles south of Panguitch, Utah) and travel to the junction of UT 12 and 63. Turn south (right) onto UT 63 and travel three miles to reach the park entrance. From the east: Travel west on UT 12 to the intersection with UT 63. Turn south (left) to reach the park entrance.

Backcountry hiking

- Located in south-central Utah
- General park information: 435/425-3791
- Hotel reservations: No lodging in the park
- Weather information: 435/425-3791 (listen for voice prompts)
- National Park Service website: www.nps.gov/care/
- Other website: www.capitolreef.org
- Fruit hotline: 435/425-3791

The Native Americans called it Land of the Sleeping Rainbow for the gorgeous colors of the cliffs, domes, and canyons. Most of the 100-mile-long Waterpocket Fold, an upheaval of rock layer also known as a monocline, lies within the national park. Capitol Reef sandstone cliffs are actually a part of this fold.

Designated a national monument in 1937, Capitol Reef was expanded to six times its original size and named a national park in 1971.

Fruit orchards with 2,500 trees thrive in Fruita, a farming area settled in the late 1800s. The Fremont Indians left behind petroglyphs and pictographs. The Petroglyph Pullout Walk winds past some of the rock art that survives.

Temple of the Moon; (inset) hiking

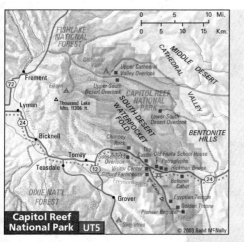

Capitol Reef National Park UT5

Best of Season

Spring-For a strenuous trek, explore the Old Wagon Trail, with panoramic views of the Waterpocket Fold along a wagon route on Miners Mountain.

Summer-Sample from the apple, cherry, pear, peach, and apricot orchards of the Fruita area when your favorite fruit is in season, from June to October.

Fall-The cottonwoods cast a golden glow in fall along Waterpocket Fold. Drive along Pleasant Creek. The 10-mile scenic drive (not a loop) from the visitors center accesses Capitol Gorge and Grand Wash, and the view of Pleasant Creek.

Winter-The Cathedral Valley area offers glittering Glass Mountain, a mound of sparkling selenite (a type of gypsum) crystals; a gypsum sinkhole nearly 50 feet across and 200 feet deep; and black lava boulders.

Drive information:
Capitol Reef National Park is located in south-central Utah on UT 24.

Framed by snowcapped cliffs and spires of evergreens, Crater Lake is the shining blue star of Crater Lake National Park. Actually the caldera of an old volcano, Crater Lake is the deepest lake in the U.S. at 1,943 feet. It is the nation's fifth oldest park, established in 1902.

Other volcanic forms surround the lake: peaks, craters, cones, and old lava flows. This was the site, thousands of years ago, of the eruption of Mount Mazama. The caldera that formed Crater Lake occurred when the volcano collapsed. It is still an area of seismic activity—almost a dozen quakes have occurred in the region since 1945. A 1993 earthquake in the park registered a magnitude of 6.0.

- Located in southwestern Oregon
- General park information: 541/594-3100
- Hotel reservations: 541/830-8700
- Weather information: Contact general park information
- National Park Service website: www.nps.gov/crla/

Crater Lake

Best of Season

Spring-Winter snows may cling to the landscape into June. At Rim Village overlook, spy the Old Man, a 30-ft. log that floats vertically, with about 4 feet showing above the lake's surface.

Summer-There's so much do in this short season, it's hard to choose. Meander Rim Drive, open only in summer, around the lake for gorgeous views and overlooks.

Fall-Visit before the snows come in October. On the lake's north side, off Cleetwood Trail, Cleetwood Cove provides about ¼-mile of rocky coastline for shore fishing with artificial bait.

Winter-Heavy snowfalls make for great snow activities. Cross-country skiing and snowshoeing opportunities abound. Snowshoes are provided for a ranger-led walk on winter ecology from Rim Village every weekend from Thanksgiving through March.

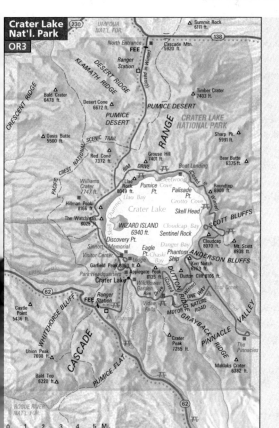

Drive information:

North: From Roseburg: OR 138 east to the park's north entrance. From Bend: US 97 south to OR 138 west to the park's north entrance. South:

From Medford: OR 62 north and east to the park's west entrance. From Klamath Falls: US 97 north to OR 62 north and west to the park's south entrance.

One of the nation's newest national parks, Cuyahoga Valley combines cultural, historical, and natural activities in one setting. Visitors can golf, fish, hike, bike, ski, bird-watch, ride a scenic railroad, explore the history of the Ohio & Erie Canal on a 20-mile towpath trail, attend concerts, and more. The Cuyahoga River, called "Crooked River" by Native Americans, winds through the 33,000-acre park. Beavers, butterflies, bats, bluegills, bass, and bullfrogs are among the many species that inhabit the park.

Located between Cleveland and Akron, the park is conveniently located from many metro areas. It was designated a national recreation area by President Gerald Ford in 1974, and elevated to national park status in 2000.

- Located between Cleveland and Akron in northeastern Ohio
- General park information: 216/524-1497
- Hotel reservations: No lodging in the park
- Weather information: Contact general park information
- National Park Service website: www.nps.gov/cuva/
- Other website: www.dayinthevalley.com

Drive information:
The park can be accessed by many different highways, including I-77, I-271, I-80 (Ohio Turnpike), and OH 8.

Best of Season

Spring-Art, music, and dance abound in the Happy Days Visitor Center all spring.

Summer-Watch an Ohio & Erie Canal lock demonstration by a costumed interpreter, then bike the 19.5-mile towpath from the Canal Visitor Center.

Fall-Check out the fall foliage from the window seat of a circa-1940 rail coach on the Cuyahoga Valley Scenic Railroad. The train runs through the heart of the park.

Winter-Near Kendall Lake Winter Sports Center, go sledding or cross-country skiing Warm up in the sports center's historic building, constructed of wormy American chestnut and sandstone.

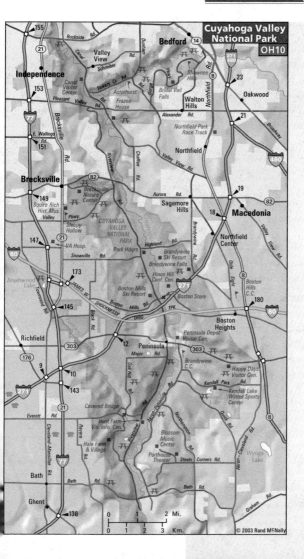

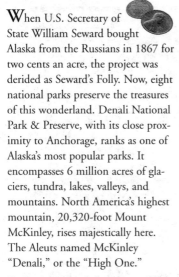

When U.S. Secretary of State William Seward bought Alaska from the Russians in 1867 for two cents an acre, the project was derided as Seward's Folly. Now, eight national parks preserve the treasures of this wonderland. Denali National Park & Preserve, with its close proximity to Anchorage, ranks as one of Alaska's most popular parks. It encompasses 6 million acres of glaciers, tundra, lakes, valleys, and mountains. North America's highest mountain, 20,320-foot Mount McKinley, rises majestically here. The Aleuts named McKinley "Denali," or the "High One."

Easily sighted and abundant wildlife spurred the creation of Denali's nickname, "the subarctic Serengeti." Visitors may catch sight of Dall's sheep, eagles, caribou, wolves, moose, even grizzly bears.

- Located in south-central Alaska
- General park information: 907/683-2294
- Hotel reservations: No lodging in the park
- Weather information: Contact general park Information
- National Park Service website: www.nps.gov/dena/

Best of Season

Spring-On a clear day in late spring, ride the Savage River shuttle bus ($2). In clear weather, Mt. McKinley may be seen in the distance at Mile 9, and the Savage River Trail affords great hiking at Mile 15. Look for caribou, wolves, and ptarmigan. Private vehicles are not permitted.

Summer-Take a ranger-led Discovery Hike and learn about grizzlies and other park wildlife. Hike topics and schedules change daily, so check ahead.

Fall-Head out after dark to view the northern lights in the night sky. Best time to view: late September through October.

Winter-Get behind a team of dogs and mush! Park concessionaires offer one-day or multi-day trips combined with camping in a heated tent. Meet the park's own dogs at the kennels building.

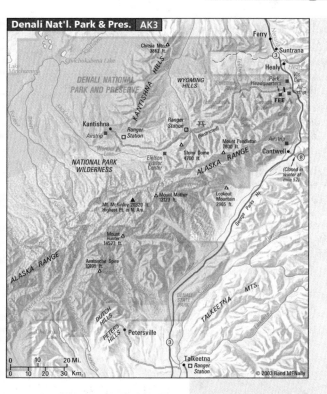

Denali Nat'l. Park & Pres. `AK3`

Ferry
Suntrana
Healy
Park Headquarters
Vis. Cen.
Air-strip
FEE

Chitsia Mtn △ 3862 ft.
Chichokabena Lake
Lake Minchumina

KANTISHNA HILLS

WYOMING HILLS

DENALI NATIONAL PARK AND PRESERVE

Ranger Station □

Kantishna
Airstrip
Ranger Station □
Wonder
(Restricted)
Mount Pendleton 1800 ft. △
Airstrip
Cantwell
(8)
Stony Dome △ 4700 ft.
Eielson Visitor Center
ALASKA RANGE
(Closed in winter at mile 52)

NATIONAL PARK WILDERNESS

△ Mount Mather 12123 ft.
Lookout Mountain 2965 ft. △

Mt. McKinley 20320 ft. ▲ Highest Pt. in N. Am.

George Parks Hwy.

Mount Hunter △ 14573 ft.

ALASKA RANGE

Avalanche Spire 10105 ft. △

TALKEETNA MTS.

DUTCH HILLS
DENALI STATE PARK
PETERS HILLS ● Petersville
(3)
Talkeetna
□ Ranger Station

0   10   20 Mi.
0 10 20 30 Km.

© 2003 Rand McNally

Mount McKinley

Drive information:
The park entrance is located along AK 3, the George Parks Highway, approximately 250 miles north of Anchorage, 125 miles south of Fairbanks, and 12 miles south of Healy. The park's mountaineering headquarters are in Talkeetna.

Private vehicles are not permitted for park road touring; a park concessionaire offers trips.

In the late 1800s, railroad passengers alighting at Belton (now West Glacier) hopped aboard a stagecoach and rode to Lake McDonald. These first tourists marked the beginning of a trend to preserve, not conquer, this postcard-perfect mountain scenery. By 1910, Glacier National Park was established, and in 1911, 4,000 people visited the park. Today, almost a century later, nearly two million people visit Glacier each year. Here, in one of the largest intact ecosystems in the continental U.S., glaciers have carved deep valleys, creating lakes of clear water.

Craggy mountain peaks, rich blue skies, ancient cedar forests, and wild-flower-dotted meadows fill the more than 1-million-acre park.

- Located in NW Montana
- General park info:
  406/888-7800
- Hotel reservations:
  406/892-2525;
  Granite Park Chalet,
  406/387-5555;
  Sperry Chalet,
  406/387-5654;
  Apgar Village Lodge,
  406/888-5484
- Weather information:
  Contact gen. park info.
- National Park Service
  website:
  www.nps.gov/glac/
- Guided tours:
  800/786-9220;
  406/892-2525

Drive information:
Access to the park from both east and west is via US 2. Park headquarters are in West Glacier.

Check with park on vehicle restrictions and road closings. Going-to-the-Sun Road is closed in spring, winter, and part of fall.

Best of Season

Spring-Spring is bird-watching time. Look for geese, loons, and kingfishers in westside forests and eastside meadows.

Summer- Hike the Highline Trail anytime from late July through early August to see a profusion of wildflowers and bear grass blooming.

Fall-Drive the winding 52-mile Going-to-the-Sun Road in early fall, crossing the Continental Divide at Logan Pass (6,646 ft.).

Winter-Drive to Lake McDonald, then strap on cross-country skis or snowshoes where the plowed road ends.

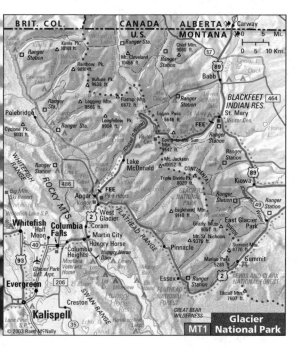

Majestic mountains of Glacier

"In the Grand Canyon, Arizona has a natural wonder which, so far as I know, is in kind absolutely unparalleled throughout the rest of the world....Keep this great wonder of nature as it is....You can not improve it. The ages have been at work on it, and man can only mar it," Theodore Roosevelt said in 1903. He went on to support the establishment of a Grand Canyon national monument, which later became part of Grand Canyon National Park.

This magnificent park, the second-most-visited after Great Smoky Mountains, is essentially divided into two sections: North Rim and South Rim. For birds, it's just 10 miles to fly across the Grand Canyon. For drivers, it's 215 miles and 5 hours in the car to go from the South Rim to the North Rim.

While it is not the deepest or widest canyon in the world (Idaho's Hells Canyon, for example, is deeper,) Grand Canyon earns its moniker from the spectacular scenery, size, and rock colors.

- Located in northern Arizona
- General park information: 928/638-7888
- Hotel reservations: 888/297-2757
- Weather information: Contact general park information
- National Park Service website: www.nps.gov/grca/

Drive information:

Grand Canyon Village (South Rim) is located 60 miles north of I-40 from Williams via AZ 64, and 80 miles northwest of Flagstaff via AZ 64/US 180. The North Rim is 44 miles south of Jacob Lake via AZ 67. Visitor services and facilities on the North Rim are only open from mid-May through mid-October.

Riding a canyon trail

Colorado River Canyon;
(inset) mule deer

Best of Season

Spring-An easy hike, the paved Rim Trail offers many vistas of the canyon. Best times are first thing in the morning, when the sun washes golden over the rocks, or late in the day, when the light turns the canyon purple and red. From April to October, watch for California condors, with 9½-foot wingspans, circling overhead.

Summer-Check out the three scenic viewpoints of the North Rim: Bright Angel Point, with views into Roaring Springs and Bright Angel Canyons; Point Imperial, the highest point on the canyon rim; and Cape Royal, with a panoramic view the length and width of the canyon.

(See map on pages 26-27)

Fall-Take advantage of cooler weather and hike Bright Angel Trail on the South Rim. Watch the rock strata change—the stretch of your fingers over a seam in this strata spans millions of years of geologic history. About ⅒-mile down, look for a sheltered rock covered with pictographs. Visit the Kolb Studio, pioneer photographers of the Grand Canyon, at the end of your trek—the studio is near the trailhead.

Winter-Stop at Yavapai Observation Station (closed for renovation 9/03 to 5/04) to learn about fossils and view the canyon. Then take the Desert View Drive (Highway 64) along the canyon rim from Grand Canyon Village to Desert View. This 26-mile drive offers many overlooks, and is open year-round.

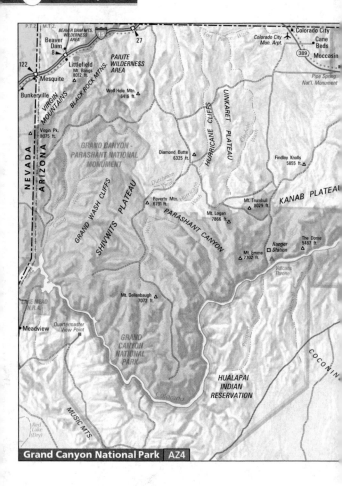

The nation's most-visited national park, Great Smoky Mountains is conveniently located near much of the country's population. Named for the smoke-like haze that often hangs over the mountains, the park has more than 800 miles of hiking and horse trails to explore in its 800 square miles. The Appalachian Trail slices right through the middle of it.

The Great Smoky Mountains are among the world's oldest, formed about 250 million years ago. Black bears, elk, deer, bats, snakes, sala- manders, wild turkey, more than 230 species of birds, and more thrive in the forested hills and valleys. First home to Native Americans, then European settlers in the 1700s and 1800s, Great Smoky Mountains gained national park status in 1934.

One of the most popular attractions is Cades Cove, with historic church- es and cabins, relics from the 19th and 20th centuries. It attracts throngs daily from April through October. The 11-mile drive around the loop road can take 2-3 hours, sometimes 4 hours, but remains a perennial favorite.

- **Located in eastern Tennessee and western North Carolina**
- **General park info: 865/436-1200**
- **Rustic lodge res.: 865/429-5704**
- **Weather information: 865/436-1200**
- **National Park Service website: www.nps.gov/grsm/**

Drive information:
Several major highways lead to the park. The following routes provide access to the three main entrances. In Tennessee: 1) From I-40 take Exit 407 (Sevierville) to TN 66 South, and continue to US 441 South. Follow US 441 to Park. 2) From I-40 in Knoxville - Exit 386B US 129 south to Alcoa/Maryville. At Maryville proceed on US 321 north through Townsend. Continue straight on TN 73 into the park. In North Carolina: From I-40, take US 19 west through Maggie Valley. Proceed to US 441 north at Cherokee into the park. From Atlanta and points south: follow US 441 and 23 north. US 441 leads to the park.

Winter weather may cause road closures, especially US 441. Check weather informa- tion before traveling.

Best of Season

Spring-Spring wildflower viewing is raised to high art level here, with an Annual Wildflower Pilgrimage.

Summer-Hike a path to one of the park's many waterfalls along the streams. A 2.4-mile round-trip walk through hemlocks off Roaring Forks Motor Nature Trail leads to Grotto Falls, the only waterfall that you can walk behind.

Fall-Savor the fall foliage on horseback. There are four commercial stables open through Thanksgiving.

Winter-In this quiet season, take the 11-mile drive through Cades Cove. While some of the summer attractions won't be open, the grist mill and visitors center are, and the peaceful solitude allows for a better appreciation of the historic nature of the area.

(See map on pages 30-31)

High-elevation mountain trail; (inset) black bear

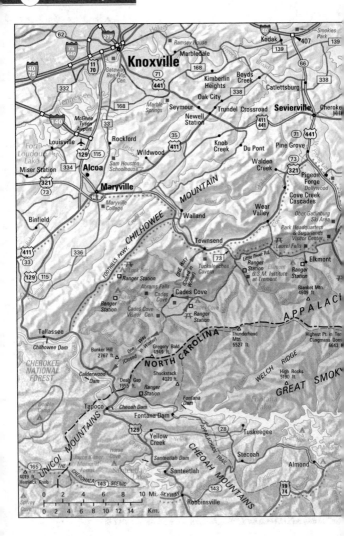

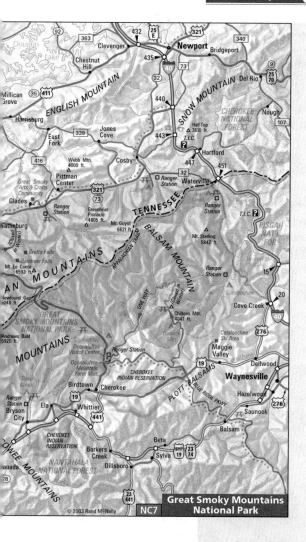

Great Smoky Mountains National Park

© 2003 Rand McNally

Lying in northern Lake Superior, Isle Royale National Park is an unspoiled wilderness. Composed of a 45-mile-long main island and numerous satellite islands, Isle Royale was sculpted by the retreat of glaciers, then mined for copper by native peoples thousands of years ago. Today, boaters cruise along the many inlets and islands, and hikers traverse more than 165 miles of trails.

With fewer annual visitors than a popular park like Yellowstone hosts in a day, there is time for solitude and communing with nature. Wildlife residents include wolf, moose, beavers, loons, snakes, and an abundance of lake trout and northern pike, among other fish.

- Located offshore from northwestern Michigan's Upper Peninsula and northeastern Minnesota
- General park information: 906/482-0984
- Hotel reservations: 270/773-2191
- Weather information: Contact general park information
- National Park Service website: www.nps.gov/isro/

Drive information:
Isle Royale National Park is accessible only by scheduled ferry, private boat, or seaplane service. There are no roads on the island, so choose your drop-off point accordingly.

Best of Season

Spring-Rent a canoe and paddle and portage from Rock Harbor Visitor Center to Lake Richie. At sunset, the waters shimmer with color. Listen for the loon, a common island migrant, calling through the forested shores.

Summer-Study the constellations while sitting on the edge of Lake Superior, the world's largest freshwater lake. Far from urban lights, the stars pop out of the night sky. If you're lucky, you may even glimpse the flowing curtains of color that make up the Aurora Borealis.

Fall-Stroll along Greenstone Ridge, the backbone of what may be the world's largest lava flow. The bright red and golden leaves of the sugar maple create a colorful carpet to soften the walk.

This park is closed in the winter.

Lake Superior shore; (inset) red fox

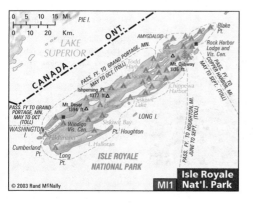

© 2003 Rand McNally

"When we try to pick out anything by itself, we find it hitched to everything else in the Universe," John Muir said in 1911, in his book, *My First Summer in the Sierra*.

Leopard lilies

Kings Canyon and Sequoia National Parks are truly a land of giants, with four of the world's five largest trees. Technically two parks, they are managed together. Sequoia was the nation's second national park, established in 1890 after Yellowstone.

But these parks are not all trees. The Sierra Nevada, a jagged granite range that runs 400 miles from northern California, cuts through the park, and there are canyons and meadows to explore.

- Located in the southern Sierra Nevada, California
- General park information: 559/565-3341
- Grant Grove Visitor Center, Kings Canyon: 559/565-4307
- Foothills Visitor Center, Sequoia: 559/565-3135
- Hotel reservations: 559/335-5500
- Weather information 559/565-3341
- National Park Service website: www.nps.gov/seki/

Drive information:

To Kings Canyon park entrance: from CA 99 at Fresno take CA 180 east approximately 1-1/4 hours.

To Sequoia park entrance: from CA 99 at Visalia take CA 198 east for approximately 1 hour.

Gasoline is NOT sold within park boundaries. Be sure to fill up in one of the towns near the park entrance. If needed, gas is also sold (albeit at much higher prices) at two locations in neighboring areas—Hume Lake (year-round) and Kings Canyon Lodge (closed in winter).

Golden trout

Best of Season

Spring-A scenic one-mile trail through Zumwalt Meadow (open mid-April) brings hikers in view of high granite walls of the mountains and close to the Kings River. In spring the meadow is surrounded by Ponderosa pine and is blooming with wildflowers such as purple lupine. Self-guiding trail booklets are available at the trailhead.

Summer-To avoid the summer crowds, head back to Mineral King, where hiking is remote, facilities primitive. Trails are steep, but trekkers are rewarded with those granite peaks, subalpine meadows, and lodgepole pine woods.

Fall-Through October, tour Crystal Cave off Generals Highway in Sequoia, discovered in 1918 by a couple of park trail construction employees. See stalactites, stalagmites, soda straws, rimstone dams, and more.

Winter-The scenic 47-mile Generals Highway that joins Kings Canyon and Sequoia is open year-round. If there's a snowstorm, it may close briefly, and tire chains are suggested. Walk back to Grant Grove to see the General Grant tree, designated the nation's Christmas tree and second in size only to the General Sherman.

(See map on pages 36-37)

Giant Sequoia trees

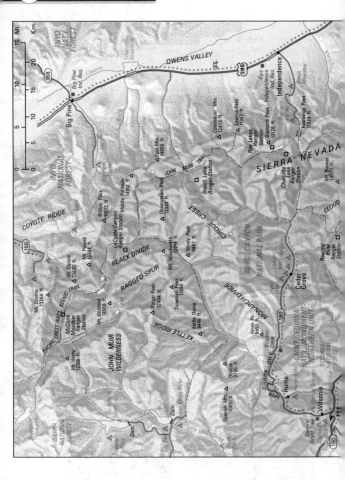

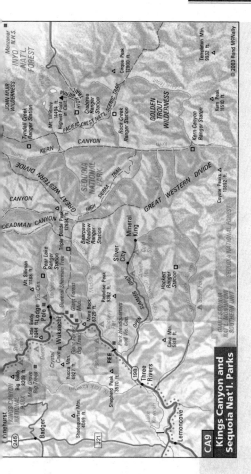

© 2003 Rand McNally

CA9

**Kings Canyon and
Sequoia Nat'l. Parks**

Manzanar N.H.S.

INYO NATL. FOREST

JOHN MUIR WILDERNESS

Tyndall Creek Ranger Station

Mt. Whitney 14494 ft. Highest Point in Calif.

Crabtree Ranger Station

HIGH

SIERRA

PACIFIC CREST NATL. SCENIC TRAIL

Cirque Peak 12900 ft.

Temdelton Mtn. 9332 ft.

MIDDLE FORK

KERN

CANYON

SEQUOIA NATIONAL PARK

GOLDEN TROUT WILDERNESS

Rock Creek Ranger Station

Kern Peak 11510 ft.

Kern Canyon Ranger Station

GREAT WESTERN DIVIDE

SIERRA TRAIL

Coyote Peaks 10892 ft.

CANYON

DEADMAN CANYON

Triple Divide Peak 12634 ft.

Bearpaw Meadow Ranger Station

HIGH

Mineral King

SEQUOIA NATL. FOREST

Pear Lake Ranger Station

Silver City

Mt. Silliman 11188 ft.

General Sherman Tree

Giant Forest Mkt.

Little Baldy 8044 ft.

Lodge Pole Vis. Cen.

Wuksachi

Paradise Peak 9362 ft.

Moro Rock 6725 ft.

Crystal Cave

Giant Forest Big Trees

Park Headquarters and Vis. Cen.

Hockett Ranger Station

Casa Mtn. 5818 ft.

GIANT SEQUOIA NATL. MONUMENT SOUTHERN UNIT

Pinehurst

KINGS CANYON NATIONAL PARK

Big Baldy 8209 ft.

Muir Grove Big Trees

Badger

Yucca Mtn. 4927 ft.

FEE

Shepherd Peak 3570 ft.

198

Three Rivers

Shadequarter Mtn. 4009 ft.

245

121

SOUTH FORK KINGS RIVER

MIDDLE FORK KAWEAH RIVER

EAST FORK KAWEAH RIVER

Lemoncove

The longest recorded cave system, Mammoth Cave was discovered by Native Americans about 4,000 years ago. Saltpeter was mined by slaves from the cave in the early 1800s for the making of gunpowder, and tours started in 1816 when it was privately owned. It became a national park in 1941.

More than 365 miles of passages have been explored, including many dry canyons and deep vertical shafts. Blind fish, crayfish, bats, and beetles live underground, some of 130 species of animals that use the cave. The main attractions for cave visitors are the rock formations: stalactites, stalagmites, gypsum flowers, flow-stone, dripstone, pits, and domes.

- Located in west-central Kentucky
- General park information: 270/758-2180
- Hotel reservations: 270/758-2225
- Weather information: Contact general park information, or www2.nature.nps.gov/ard/parks/maca/macacam/macacam.htm for the park's webcam
- National Park Service website: www.nps.gov/maca/

River Styx spring; (inset) daffodil

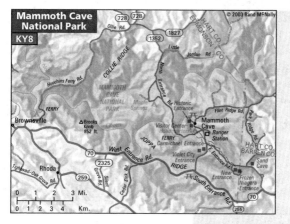

Mammoth Cave National Park
KY8

© 2003 Rand McNally

Best of Season

Spring-Follow coal-oil lanterns into the area of the saltpeter mining operation, large rooms and passageways on a strenuous, 3-hour Violet City Lantern Tour. You'll also see the remains of a tuberculosis hospital—an experiment gone awry, as the cool, confined cave air proved counterproductive to patients.

Summer-While the crowds are underground, cast your line from shore for pan fish—crappie, bluegill, and bass will be biting. No fishing license is needed.

Fall-Take a gentle hike on the rolling hills, or launch a canoe on the Green River. Scenic boat rides run through October.

Winter-Adventurers should sign up in advance for the ranger-guided Wild Cave Tour. The six-hour tour ends in lit cave sections.

Drive information:

The most direct route south from Louisville, KY is I-65 south to Exit 53 at Cave City. Another 15 minutes of driving will bring you to the park visitor center. The most direct route north from Nashville, TN is I-65 north to Exit 48 at Park City, KY. Another 10 minutes of driving will bring you to the park visitor center. Nashville and the park are both in the Central Time Zone. Louisville is in the Eastern Time Zone, one hour ahead of the park.

Established in 1906, Mesa Verde protects the works of people, not nature: the pre-Columbian cliff dwellings of the ancestral Puebloans. Covering 52,073 acres in Colorado, in a land of piñon and juniper, canyons and mesas, the park preserves the homes of a people that migrated south in the late 1200s.

There are more than 5,000 archeological sites in the park, and of these about 600 are cliff alcove sites. Visitors can join ranger-guided tours of the dwellings or visit on their own, peruse museum exhibits, hike (with permits), go cross-country skiing, bird-watch, and watch evening slide programs at the campground, among other pursuits.

- Located in south-western Colorado
- General park information: 970/529-4465
- Hotel reservations: 800/449-2288
- Weather information: Contact general park information
- National Park Service website: www.nps.gov/meve

Drive information:
The park museum is a one-hour drive from Cortez, Colorado, heading east on US 160 to the park turnoff, and a 1.5-hour drive from Durango, Colorado, heading west on US 160 to the park turnoff.

Best of Season

Spring-Drive the Mesa Top Loop Road. Twelve easily accessed sites along the route include surface dwellings and overlooks, such as Sun Point Overlook and Sun Temple.

Summer-Register at the trailhead to hike Petroglyph Point Trail. It winds from Spruce Tree House trail up to the canyon rim, then along the rim back to the museum. The hike affords great views of Spruce Tree and Navajo canyons.

Fall-Take a ranger-guided tour of Cliff Palace or Balcony House. Cliff Palace, the largest cliff dwelling, and Balcony House, with outstanding architectural detail, are the most popular tours, and may be less crowded in fall.

Winter-Stop at Park Point overlook (8,572 ft.) at sunset to view four states: Arizona, Utah, New Mexico, and Colorado. In the distance, rising about 1,800 ft. above the plain on the Navajo Indian Reservation, Shiprock peak glows in the light.

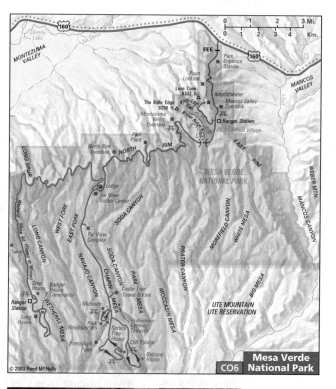

Mesa Verde
National Park
CO6

© 2003 Rand McNally

Cliff Palace

Native Americans called the peak Takhoma, and avoided the spirits there. Mount Rainier, with 26 major or named glaciers, is the fifth-highest peak in the lower 48 U.S. states. Thousands of people climb to the 14,410-foot summit annually. The park covers 235,625 acres, threaded with hiking trails, meadows, and snowfields.

Paradise Valley, filled with snow in winter, is a beautiful meadow in summer. John Muir called it "...the most extravagantly beautiful of all the alpine gardens I ever beheld in all my mountain-top wanderings."

Summer is time for hiking, climbing, and listening to evening ranger talks, while winter is filled with skiing, snowshoeing, and sledding.

- Located in south-central Washington
- General park information: 360/569-2211
- Hotel reservations: 360/569-2275
- Weather information: Contact general park information
- National Park Service website: www.nps.gov/mora/

Drive information:
Year-round access to the park is via WA 706 to the Nisqually Entrance in the SW corner of the park. Limited winter access is available via WA 123 in the SE corner of the park. The Carbon River/Mowich Lake area (NW corner) is accessed via WA 165 through Wilkeson. Summer access is available via WA 410 and WA 123 on the N and E sides of the park.

Best of Season

Spring-Elk migrate in spring, and wildlife-watching is prime. Try the steep Shriner Peak Trail. There's no shade, but the views of Mount Rainier, the Ohanapecosh Valley, and the Cascades are incomparable.

Summer-Hike through sub-alpine meadows to view Nisqually Glacier, learning about crevasses, moraines, and seracs.

Fall-Even a novice can aspire to the heights through a one-day climbing school course. Clamp on ice crampons and get instruction in ice-axe arrest, roped glacier travel, even the basics of walking and breathing.

Winter-Paradise is one of the snowiest places on earth. When eight inches of snow pack the ground, innertubes and plastic sleds begin to fly down the hills of the snowplay area.

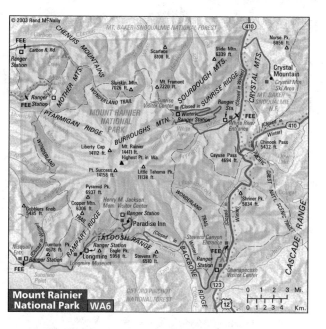

Mount Rainier; (inset) picnicking

First there is the rain, and then more rain, or maybe snow—some 200 inches of precipitation annually fall on Olympic National Park. With magnificent mountains, active glaciers, a wild and scenic coastline, and Olympic-sized trees in old-growth forests spread over nearly 1 million acres, no wonder millions visit this national park annually. It is an easy drive from Seattle or Tacoma.

The park has numerous Douglas fir, which can grow to 300 feet, as well giant Western red cedar, Sitka spruce, and Western hemlock, at up to 150-175 feet. Activities include hiking through old-growth forests along the Skokomish River, listening to the surf at Rialto Beach, hiking to view glaciers, and watching for Roosevelt elk, Olympic marmot, and black bears.

Best of Season

Spring-In late spring, take a walk in the Hoh Rainforest. After a rain, the forest floor wiggles alive with big yellow banana slugs seeking out mushrooms. These monster-sized (up to 10 inches) slimy creatures are native to the area, the densest population of slugs in the world.

Summer-Take advantage of the warmer weather and raft the Elwha River. View forests and mountain peaks topped with snow.

- Located in northwestern Washington
- General park information: 360/565-3000
- Hotel reservations:
  Kalaloch Lodge,
  360/962-2271

  Lake Crescent Lodge,
  360/928-3211

  Log Cabin Resort,
  360/928-3325

  Sol Duc Hot Springs
  Resort, 360/327-3583
- Weather information:
  Contact gen. park info.
- Park Service website:
  www.nps.gov/olym/

Drive information:
From the Seattle/Tacoma area, travelers may reach US 101 by several different routes, either by crossing Puget Sound on one of the Washington State Ferries or by driving south around the Sound. Travel time along any of these routes is approximately two-and-a-half to three hours from the Seattle/Tacoma area to Port Angeles, where the main park visitor center and park headquarters are located.

Fall-Wade in the Hole in the Wall tidal pools, searching for sea creatures such as starfish and anemones.

Winter-At 5,200 feet, there's usually plenty of snow at Hurricane Ridge. Try tubing, sledding, even skiing.

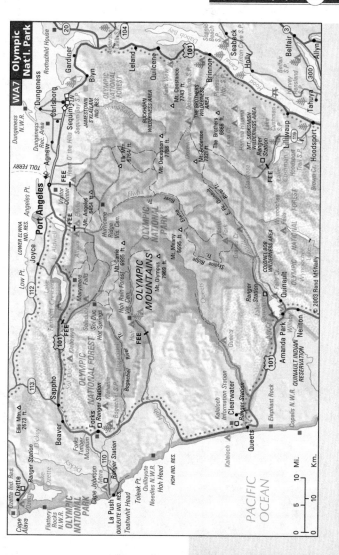

© 2003 Rand McNally

About 225 million years ago, a forest grew in the highlands above marshes and streams in what is present-day Arizona. Now this area receives about nine inches of rainfall annually, and summers are hot and shadeless. What is left are forests of petrified wood, small and great huge chunks of former logs, some more than 100 feet long. These are the remains of giant trees that were buried in sediment and volcanic ash and became petrified before being exposed by erosion.

- Located in east-central Arizona
- General park information: 928/524-6228
- Hotel reservations: No lodging in the park
- Weather information: Contact general park information
- National Park Service website: www.nps.gov/pefo/

It is a colorful scene, with multi-hued badlands and the Painted Desert's banded sedimentary layers formed from various minerals. Green collared lizards scamper among the rocks.

Most visitors simply drive the 28-mile main road through the 93,533-acre park, stopping at various petrified forest spots.

Giant petrified log; (inset) pronghorns

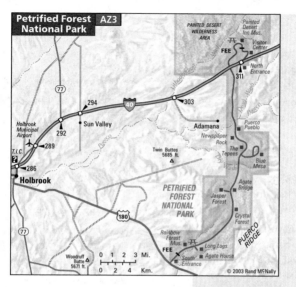

Petrified Forest National Park AZ3

© 2003 Rand McNally

Best of Season

Spring-Scenic turnouts along the drive offer views of the Painted Desert and badland formations. Stop to wander among the ancestral Puebloans ruins in the desert and bird-watch for white-face ibis, cinnamon teal, and peregrine falcon.

Summer-Head to the Rainbow Forest museum. Pieces of petrified wood that visitors carried out of the park and then returned are exhibited, along with stories of bad luck that befell the pilferers.

Fall-Hike into the Wilderness Area from Kachina Point. There are no designated trails, but 43,000 acres to explore.

Winter-Check out the ranger program at Rainbow Forest Museum in the morning and an afternoon program at the park's north end.

Drive information:

Petrified Forest stretches between I-40 and US 180. Visitors traveling west on I-40 should exit at milepost 311, drive through the park and connect with US 180 at the south end. Take US 180 to Holbrook to continue west on I-40. Eastbound visitors should exit I-40 at Holbrook and take US 180 to the park's south entrance. Drive north through the park to return to I-40.

"**M**agnificent mountains in the sky, peak after peak along the horizon—an inspiring skyline—such is the setting of Rocky Mountain National Park. From one hundred miles distant, out on the plains of Colorado or Wyoming, these snowy, rugged mountain tops give one a thrill as they appear to join with the cloud and form a horizon that seems to be a part of the scenery of the sky," wrote Enos Mills, the "John Muir of the Rockies," in the early 1900s.

The snowy mountaintops still seem to touch the sky, with Longs Peak reaching 14,255 feet. Trail Ridge Road, which climbs to 12,183 feet, is the highest place you can travel by car in the national parks. Even the valleys are at a lofty 8,000 feet. This park is home to bighorn sheep, bear, elk, moose, beaver, mule deer, and of course, eagles and hawks.

More than three million people visit the park annually to hike, climb, bike, ride horseback, bird-watch, ski, fish, and just sightsee. Free shuttle buses run along Bear Lake corridor, connecting trailheads and parking areas, making it easy to get on a trail.

(continued on pages 50-51)

- Located in north-central Colorado
- General park info: 970/586-1206
- Campground reservations: 800/365-2267; Back country, primitive camping: 970/586-1242
- Hotel reservations: No lodging in the park
- Weather information: Contact general park information
- National Park Service website: www.nps.gov/romo/

Drive information:
Via US 34, US 36 from the east through Estes Park, Colorado and from I-70 and US 40 to US 34 through Granby and Grand Lake.

Golden-mantled ground squirrel

Cub Lake; (inset) fly tying

Yellow stonecrop wildflowers

Big Thompson River; (inset) biking

Best of Season

Spring-Look for wildlife. Elk are at lower elevations in the spring, winter, and fall, and can be seen in meadows, especially at feeding times—dawn and dusk.

Summer-Take Trail Ridge Road to the summit. Many paths lead to alpine flowers that have taken decades to develop.

Fall-Bring a picnic lunch and hike the Longs Peak trail to Chasm Lake and the base of Longs Peak. Keep your food covered until you're ready to eat, though: If you leave your sandwich out too long, marmots will sneak out to steal it!

Winter-The park's wetter west side gets the brunt of snowfall, so cross-country skiers and snowshoers should head there. Reservations are suggested for ranger-led snowshoe treks on weekends in the Kawuneeche Valley.

Fishing

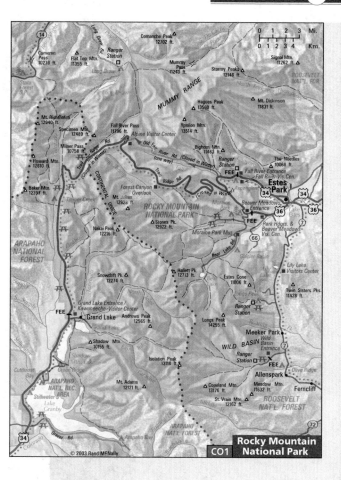

Rocky Mountain
National Park
CO1
© 2003 Rand McNally

Set in a 70-mile stretch of the Blue Ridge Mountains, Shenandoah National Park was established in 1935 after ten years of private land acquisition. The area had been logged and farmed since the 1700s, and stone foundations and cemeteries are reminders of the mountain people that lived here.

To many visitors, the 105-mile Skyline Drive defines the park, with 75 scenic overlooks into valleys and forested hills. Hiking trails—more than 500 miles—cover the park, including 101 miles of the famed Appalachian Trail.

Rich, varied wildlife thrives in the oak/hickory hardwood forests, from deer and bears to bobcats, raccoons, and groundhogs.

Harry F. Byrd, Sr., a former Virginia governor and U.S. senator, frequented the park to climb its many peaks. "In the tragedies and other strains of our modern world, generations to come will receive a peace of mind and new hopes in lifting their eyes to the peaks and canyons of the Shenandoah National Park," he said.

- Located in the Blue Ridge Mountains in northern Virginia
- General park info: 540/999-3500
- Hotel reservations: 800/999-4714
- Potomac Appalachian Trail Club Cabins: 703/242-0693
- Weather information: Contact general park information
- National Park Service website: www.nps.gov/shen/

Drive information:
The four entrances to the park are via I-66 and US 340 to the north entrance at Front Royal, US 211 to the central entrance at Thornton Gap, US 33 to Swift Run Gap, and I-64 to the Rockfish Gap entrance at the southern end of the park and the northern end of the Blue Ridge Parkway. Speed limit for Skyline Drive is 35 mph.

Eastern box turtle; (inset) Eastern tiger swallowtail

*Bearface Mountain;
(inset) mushrooms*

Best of Season

Spring-The best time to travel Skyline Drive is in the spring, when wildflowers first bloom, then trees leaf out. Look for violets and hepatica in March and April; dogwoods, magnolias, and redbuds in May.

Summer-Watch for butterflies in Big Meadow. Monarchs, fritillaries, sulphurs, and swallowtails flock to the milkweed and blooming flowers here.

Fall-Hike down from Skyline Drive to Rapidan Camp, when the leaves are in full color. Rapidan Camp is a presidential retreat, built by President Herbert Hoover and his wife, that predates Camp David, with 1920s- and 30s-era cabins, rarely used. Bring lunch and picnic atop logs near the trout stream that runs through the center of the camp.

Winter-The crowds are gone, and all facilities are closed, but if there's ample snow and Skyline Drive is open, dust off the snowshoes and head out for a trek on hiking trails and fire roads.

(See map on pages 54-55)

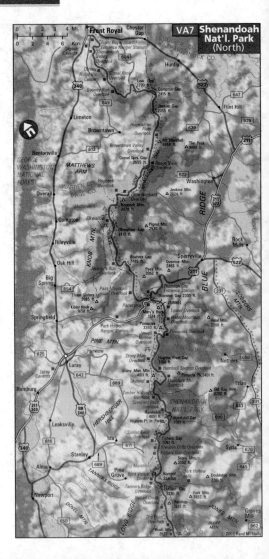

VA7 **Shenandoah Nat'l. Park** (North)

© 2003 Rand McNally

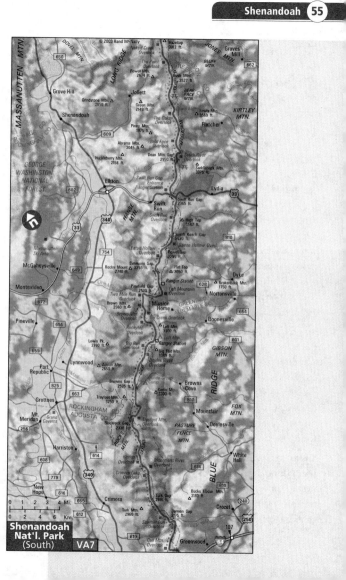

Shenandoah
Nat'l. Park
(South)   VA7

"Climb the mountains and get their good tidings. Nature's peace will flow into you as sunshine flows into trees. The winds will blow their own freshness into you, and the storms their energy, while cares will drop off like autumn leaves," John Muir said of Yellowstone. The grand-daddy of them all, Yellowstone was established in 1872 by President Ulysses S. Grant as the world's first national park. It's also one of the more popular, with nearly three million annual visitors. Many come just to see the park's most famous attraction, Old Faithful Geyser, which erupts about every 80 minutes.

There are more geysers and hot springs here—some 10,000—than the rest of the world combined. This amazing park boasts the largest concentration of free-roaming wildlife in the lower 48 U.S. states, including the only place where bison have roamed continuously since prehistoric times.

Visitors enjoy hiking, climbing, biking, fishing, boating, bird-watching, skiing, snowmobiling, stargazing, and just plain driving in this 2.2-million-acre park.

- Located in northwestern Wyoming, southwestern Montana, and eastern Idaho
- General park info: 307/344-7381
- Hotel reservations: 307/344-7311
- Weather information: 307/344-2113
  Roads: 307/344-2117
- National Park Service website: www.nps.gov/yell/
- Bus tours: 307/344-7311

Drive information:
North Entrance - Via US 89, near the gateway community of Gardiner, MT, the North Entrance is the only park entrance open all year.

West Entrance - Via US 20 adjacent to the town of West Yellowstone, MT, the West Entrance is open to wheeled vehicles from the third Friday in April through the first Sunday in November.

South Entrance - Via US 89/US 287/US191 and **East Entrance** - Via US20/US14/US16 are open from the first Friday of May through the first Sunday in November.

Northeast Entrance - Via US 212, near the gateway community of Cooke City, MT, this entrance is open year-round for access to Cooke City through Gardiner, MT and the North Entrance.

Lower Yellowstone Falls

Best of Season

Spring-Take a course in wolf conservation and management from the Yellowstone Association Institute at Lamar Buffalo Ranch. Learn about gray wolves, and go wolf-watching.

Summer-Tread the lightly visited Pelican Creek trail in Pelican Valley from June through September. Grizzlies and wolves are sometimes spotted there. Check at the Yellowstone Lake ranger station for current trail information and backcountry permits.

Fall-Bring your bike to traverse the abandoned railbed (secondary dirt road) in the Mammoth area paralleling the Yellowstone River.

Winter-Climb aboard a snowcoach—a sort of minibus on skis—for a warm winter tour of the park and a chance to spot wildlife.

(See map on page 59)

Pool at Upper Geyser Basin

Rising precipitously above the Snake River plain, the jagged spires of the Teton Range jab towards the sky. This mountain range commands the scenery of Grand Teton National Park, which also include Jackson Hole valley and 50 miles of the Snake River. Peaks ranging from about 11,000 to 13,000 feet have names that speak of their history. Grand Teton, the highest in the range at 13,770 feet, was named by French trappers. Static Peak got its name from the fact that it's frequently struck by lightning. Teewinot Mountain, over Cascade Canyon, is derived from the Shoshone word "many pinnacles."

Because most visitors pour into the park from Memorial Day to Labor Day, summer is the height of activity.

Best of Season
Spring-In late spring, wildflowers begin to bloom, starting in the valley. The color works its way upward as the days grow warmer. Look for bluebells, daisies, Indian paintbrush, lupines, and more.

Summer-Raft the Snake River, or head to the marshy Willow Flats Turnout, a hangout for birds, beaver, and moose. Best times for seeing moose: dawn or dusk.

Fall-Hop on a bicycle and tool along secondary roads in Antelope Flats and Kelly Area for

- Located in northwestern Wyoming
- General park information: 307/739-3300
- Hotel reservations: 800/628-9988 or 307/543-3100; 800/672-6012 or 307/543-2831
- Weather information: Contact general park information
- Park Service website: www.nps.gov/grte/

Drive information:
East and north from Salt Lake City, UT, east from Boise, ID, or south from western Montana, to Idaho Falls, ID, and over Teton Pass or up the Snake River Canyon to Jackson, WY, then north 12 miles to the Moose Visitor Center. Or west from Riverton, WY, or Casper, WY, over Togwotee Pass and into the park via the east entrance. Or south from Yellowstone National Park and through Grand Teton's north entrance.

great views of the mountains and golden aspen leaves.

Winter-Though many parks have banned snowmobiling, it is still permitted in Grand Teton. Follow the Continental Divide Snowmobiling Trail from the east park boundary alongside the highway to the south entrance of Yellowstone.

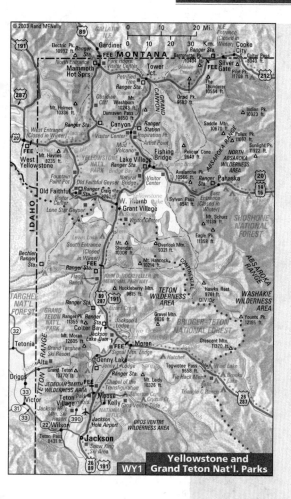

Yellowstone and
Grand Teton Nat'l. Parks

WY1

Nearly 4 million visitors annually flock to Yosemite, with almost half a million a month in the peak summer season. There's lots to see, with 263 miles of roads and 800 miles of hiking trails to explore, as well as waterfalls, giant sequoias, El Capitan, Half Dome, peregrine falcons, owls, eagles, and mule deer. The most popular trek, Mist Trail, starts at Happy Isles, runs along the Merced River and passes Vernal Fall (317 ft.) and Nevada Fall (594 ft.). The park offers living history programs, nature walks and talks, even sightseeing tours on trams. Good bets: an actor's portrayal of John Muir in Yosemite Village, or the Jackson Hole Wildlife Film Festival award-winning park film "Spirit of Yosemite" in the Visitor Center auditorium.

- Located in California's Sierra Nevada
- General park information: 209/372-0200
- Hotel reservations: 559/252-4848
- Weather information: 209/372-0200
- National Park Service website: www.nps.gov/yose/
- Other websites: www.yosemite.com www.yosemite.org

Best of Season

Spring-See a lunar rainbow from the bridge at the base of Lower Yosemite Fall on a full moon night.

Summer-Head out early to hike to the top of Half Dome via the John Muir trail or take a sightseeing tour, as some are not available in other seasons, such as the moonlight tour.

Fall-Bike in the east end of Yosemite, near Happy Falls and Mirror Lake.

Winter-Check out "snow cones" at the base of Upper Yosemite, formed by frozen spray blowing down from the waterfall.

El Capitan, Merced River

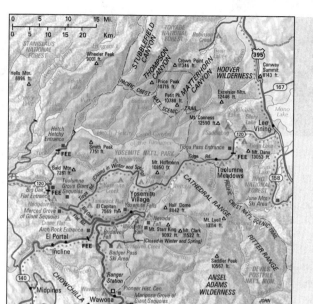

Yosemite
CA8 National Park
© 2003 Rand McNally

Drive information:
There are four entrances to the park: South entrance on CA 41 north from Fresno; Arch Rock entrance on CA 140 east from Merced; Big Oak Flat entrance on CA 120 east from Modesto and Manteca; Tioga Pass entrance on CA 120 west from Lee Vining and US 395.

The Tioga Pass entrance is closed from the first major snowstorm in November until late May to June due to snow.

All other park entrances are kept open all year, but may require tire chains because of snow anytime between November and April.

Virgin River

- Located in southwestern Utah
- General park info: 435/772-3256
- Hotel reservations: 303/297-2757
- Weather information: Contact general park information
- National Park Service website: www.nps.gov/zion/

Carved canyons, cliffs, and mesas of southern Utah form the 229 square miles of Zion National Park. Zion, which means "place of refuge" in Hebrew, offers jaw-dropping views with every turn in the road, such as sandstone cliffs that are among the highest in the world. In the Kolob Canyons section of the park, 17 miles south of Cedar City, the afternoon light reflecting off the walls of the Finger Canyons turns all that it touches a glowing orange.

Puebloan peoples once lived here, growing corn and other crops. Their pictographs and petroglyphs remain in a few places in the park. In the Zion Human History Museum, photographs and artifacts of early residents, including ancestral Puebloans, southern Paiutes, and Mormon pioneers, are on exhibit. An overview film of the park can be seen in the museum.

Best of Season

Spring-Take the 10-mile scenic Zion-Mt. Carmel Highway through tunnels and steep switchbacks to Checkerboard Mesa, with its weathered sandstone.

Summer-Feel as tiny as an ant when you hike through the Narrows, just six yards wide with thousand-foot-high walls. Check at the visitor center for weather conditions before starting this hike.

Fall-Take a hike to revel in the jewel-toned fall leaves. The color show begins with the aspens, moving into the hardwood forests, and finally the cottonwoods in Zion Canyon.

Winter-Winter is mild in Zion, and hiking is possible on the Southwest Desert Chinle trail, and the Coalpits and Huber Washes.

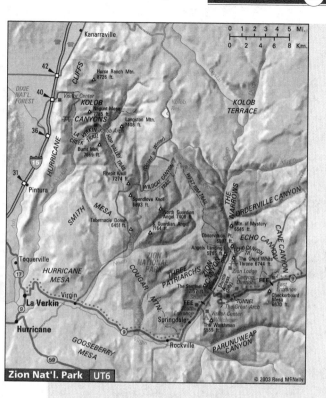

Zion Nat'l. Park   UT6

© 2003 Rand McNally

Drive information:

I-15 passes west of the park and connects with UT 9 and UT 17 to the park. US 89 passes east and connects with UT 9 to the park. The Zion Canyon Visitor Center is a short distance from the park's South Entrance, which is adjacent to Springdale. The Zion Human History Museum is 1 mile from the South Entrance. The Visitor Center at the Kolob Canyons entrance is accessible from I-15, exit 40.

Although private vehicles can be driven through the park at any time, the Upper Zion Canyon section is accessible only by free shuttle bus from April through October.

Park listings by state.
Alphabetical listings in Table of Contents, on page 1.

Alaska

Denali 20-21

Arizona

Grand Canyon 24-27
Petrified Forest 46-47

California

Kings Canyon 34-37
Sequoia 34-37
Yosemite 60-61

Colorado

Mesa Verde 40-41
Rocky Mountain 48-51

Kentucky

Mammoth Cave 38-39

Maine

Acadia 6-7

Michigan

Isle Royale 32-33

Montana

Glacier 22-23

North Carolina

Great Smoky
Mountains 28-31

Ohio

Cuyahoga Valley 18-19

Oregon

Crater Lake 16-17

Tennessee

Great Smoky
Mountains 28-31

Texas

Big Bend 10-11

Utah

Arches 8-9
Bryce Canyon 12-13
Capitol Reef 14-15
Zion 62-63

Virginia

Shenandoah 52-55

Washington

Mount Rainier 42-43
Olympic 44-45

Wyoming

Grand Teton 58-59
Yellowstone 56-57,59

*Rocky
Mountain
National
Park*